21 Ways To Attract, Retain, & Engage Millennials

Gary Wilbers

Coach | Trainer | Keynote Speaker | Author

Copyright © 2017 Gary Wilbers
All rights reserved.
ISBN:
ISBN-13:

DEDICATION

I dedicate this book to the five business executives with whom I had an interesting discussion about the challenges millennials present.

https://goascend.biz/millennial-effect-learn-more

Congratulations on taking the first step to attract, retain & engage millennials.

With our new twelve video online training series, The Millennial Effect, you will have the competitive advantage by recognizing the millennials' differences and learning to adjust for their weaknesses while utilizing their many strengths. In less than two hours you will implement these strategies into your company.

The Millennial Effect is available on my website for $497.
Right now you can get it for only $297 plus our coaching program FREE of charge.

Coaching For Success (value $197) is a five video training series that will give you the results you're looking for to quickly coach not only the millennials but your entire team.

With our 30-day money back guarantee, you have nothing to lose but so much to gain. ONLY $297 ($694 retail value).

https://goascend.biz/millennial-effect-learn-more

CONTENTS

Introduction   Pg. 8

Attracting Millennials   **Pg. 10**

Retaining Millennials   **Pg. 23**

Engaging Millennials   **Pg. 36**

Conclusion   Pg. 47

INTRODUCTION

"Your mindset will determine how you will impact the culture of your company to attract, retain and engage the millennial generation." – Gary Wilbers

I was listening to five business executives discussing the challenges of dealing with younger workers (millennials) and complaining about their lack of work ethics. The executives felt as though this generation did not understand their business practices because the millennials had new and different expectations that the executives had not dealt with before.

The challenge today is not the millennial worker, but how we decide to view this generation. Each generation has had trade-offs. Just think about what your parents thought of your generation compared to their generation. I have read in multiple publications that each generation is different and unique. The key is how to harness the strengths of that generation in order to help them understand what is expected in the workforce.

As a coach and speaker I share with my audiences that the way we view this millennial generation will determine our success or failure in the future. In the next several years this generation will become the largest generation in the workforce. Your approach and strategies to attract, retain and engage the millennial worker will determine your success in business for years to come.

This book will give you seven strategies for each of these areas. As you read this book, I want you to think about your company and what you are doing in each of these three areas. My goal in writing this book is to help you create a plan that will not only bring millennials into your company but also help them to become more successful. With the number of baby boomers retiring, it is vital that you train and develop the millennials to become the next level of leaders in your company.

Your future success depends on the millennials.

COPYRIGHT: <A HREF="HTTPS://WWW.123RF.COM/PROFILE_CHEREZOFF">CHEREZOFF / 123RF STOCK PHOTO</A>

ATTRACTING MILLENNIALS

"Creating recruiting strategies that attract the millennial worker is your number one business priority. This will guarantee your future success." – Gary Wilbers

Millennials are becoming the largest generation in the workforce and having successful attraction strategies will ensure you are an employer that millennials want to work for. Here are seven strategies for attracting millennials:

1. RECRUITING STRATEGIES

As you decide what recruiting strategies to use when attracting millennials, try to think like them. You may need to survey other millennials that work for you about what they look for when they are seeking employment. You need to be open to new ways of recruiting this generation. Here are several ways for recruiting millennials:

On-line Job Postings: Find out what the hottest job board postings in your market are. From researching you will find which on-line postings will work best within your market. Each business will be different depending on the type of person you are recruiting. Here are the top sites for job listings:

- Indeed is the most popular job posting site with over 180 million unique visitors each month. It offers free, paid, pay-per-job, and pay-per-click postings. The price is approximately $10 pay-per-click. It works with all industries and job types.

- LinkedIn is the most popular social network for professionals and provides paid and paid-per-job posts. The ability to target the correct audience makes it easier to reach your ideal candidates. It is mostly used for white-collar jobs. The pricing is determined by your location.

- Monster has a lot of web traffic and offers paid and pay-per-job posts. The price is usually around $130-$400 per post. It provides a great resume database.

- CareerBuilder is one of the most trafficked job sites in the United States. It allows for paid and pay-per-job posts that average around $250-$400 per post.

I have had great success by offering an incentive to our team members for referral of a new hire. If the person they referred came on board, the team member would receive an incentive. If the referral stayed with us for three months, six months and twelve months, the team member received a bonus at each stage. Your good team members will only refer people who they think will truly be productive. The team member realizes if the referral is not a good fit, it will create challenges not only for the company but also for him/her. The key to this strategy is the millennial must think your company is a great place to work or he/she will not share with his/her network.

2. SOCIAL MEDIA

Social media is the new norm. It is not only a marketing tool for generating business but also a tool for recruiting new team members. The amount of time spent each day on social media is nearly two hours. How can you use the time spent on social media to attract the millennials you want working for your company?

The use of social media to recruit new team members can be done several ways: One of the first things you can do is use your LinkedIn, Facebook, Instagram, Twitter, and other sites to post the opening of the position you have available. If you have company pages, post on these also. Make sure you have a place on your website for directly linking to the position and job description. Make sure the candidates can apply online for the positions. If they have to email or mail you a resume, you will decrease the number of potential candidates. The question to ask is "Is my company current on the use of technology?" If not, this will detract potential millennials from joining your company.

Another way is to ask team members to post about the positions you have available in your company. Find a way to create an incentive for the referring team member. If you expand your network to include your team's network, you will be reaching a larger potential candidate pool.

The last way to use social media is to target your potential prospects by paying for ads. You can pay for a demographic that would most likely fit your ideal candidate's profile. The use of social media can greatly enhance the number of potential candidates.

3. PURPOSE

Why would you want to identify your company's purpose when you are attracting millennials? The millennial generation is searching for companies with a purpose. Purpose is defined as "the reason for which something is done or created or for which something exists." This means the millennials want to know why your company exists and how your company benefits society. I used to be in the wireless industry. We felt our purpose was connecting our customer to his/her world. What did this mean to the customer? For example, To my mother this meant she could connect with her two living sisters: one lived in Ohio and the other in Kansas City, MO. She could talk to each of them every day because it was no longer a long-distance phone call. This was important to my mother because as she aged, she wanted to connect more with her family.

Here is a suggestion: Take time with your team and let them help you define the company's purpose. Ask the following questions:

- What is the primary reason your company exists?

- What do we do that benefits our customers?

- Why?

As you define your purpose, make sure this is connected with the vision, mission and core values of your company. When your team understands the purpose of your company, you will see that they are able to find new, creative solutions when you are trying to improve your processes. The key reason behind finding your purpose is that it will create a higher level of engagement from all of your team members.

4. BEHAVIOR-BASED QUESTIONS

Millennials have a different set of skills and experiences than any other generations. When you interview millennials, they are willing to be more open and honest than other generations. You can use this transparency in the interviewing process. One of the keys is to use behavior-based interview questions that many companies now use in the workplace. Behavior-based questions are used in the interview process for identifying how the interviewee would act or behave in common-employment-related situations.

The key to success in behavior-based questions is to define the core competencies needed for the position. When you know these competencies, you will be able to ask behavior-based questions. This allows the interviewer to know how the interviewee handled the situation instead of hypothetically addressing the problem. Behavior-based questions are more specific, probing, and direct than traditional-interview questions. Here are some suggestions for behavior-based questions:

- Provide an example of how you worked with a team in the past.

- When you have had a tight deadline, how did you handle the workload?

- Provide an example of how you would handle a difficult team member or boss.

- Identify a time you had to use problem solving to create a solution for a difficult problem.

- Share a goal you reached and how you attained it.

Any behavior-based questions can be used for any candidate. You will find most millennials are willing to share more information with you than the other generations. The objective of any great interview using behavioral-based questions is to allow the candidate to share his/her experiences in order for you to determine if he/she is a fit in your company. The more you allow the candidate to speak, the more you will ascertain about him/her. Remember: Make the candidate feel at ease, and make the interview conversational instead of a structured, rigid process.

5. EXPECTATIONS & ASSUMPTIONS

As I work with companies seeking to attract the right candidates, I have noticed that setting the expectations and assumptions with the candidate helps him/her to be successful. I believe this starts with the interview and continues during the onboarding process. I think too many companies do not set the expectations of what a new hire is supposed to do. Then when he/she comes onboard, the new hire thinks the employer has not been transparent with him/her. Make sure to take time in the interview process to explain in detail what the position truly requires. It also is the time to find out what the potential employee assumes about the position.

One very successful method I have seen utilized in the interview process is to include a peer. Use the peer to review what he/she believes the expectations of this position are. This will generate great discussion with the candidate. It will also show the value of the team member by having him/her involved with the hiring process. Too often companies do not allow the front line to be part of the hiring process, but these are the individuals who will help determine if the new team member is successful. The key is to change your hiring practices from human resources to everyone in the company. The more you create a team-hiring practice, the quicker you will see everyone become involved in finding solutions for attracting the best candidates.

You will increase your success with candidates by setting the expectations. However, if you can figure out a way to help a candidate with the assumptions he/she has about the position, it gives each party a win-win. One creative approach I observed is to ask the candidate before he/she begins the new position if he/she would like to observe someone in the same role as he/she will be. This takes an extra effort on everyone's part. The key is to make hiring and onboarding everyone's job. One company that used this creative approach has reduced its turnover by more than 70%. In the long run this reduces the expenses of a company.

6. CULTURE

Did you know your company's culture determines how successful you will be in attracting not only millennials but every other generation in the workforce? It has been long publicized that Google has created a culture that helps them attract the best and brightest talent. How do you create a culture that will attract the type of people you are looking for? Here are three ways you can create a culture that not only attracts but also retains and engages your team members:

- Create an online survey asking your team members to describe what characteristics of attitudes, values, goals and practices are prevalent in your company.

- Appoint a team of people from all levels of the company to review the responses, hire a facilitator to moderate the discussion to determine the most important characteristics of your culture, and share with your company.

- Survey your team again in order to find out if you are missing something from your current culture that they would like to see in the future. Share with your team. Using step 2 discuss and then proceed to develop your company's culture. Engage your team to create a statement about your company's culture.

The main challenge in creating a culture statement is that it can only happen by allowing your team to design the culture of your company. Management's role is to help provide the resources to facilitate the culture which must come from the team. The success of your culture lies within your team.

7. TRAINING & DEVELOPMENT

The millennial worker has the mindset of wanting on-going learning from their company in order for the continuation of growing and developing his/her skills. Most millennials are looking for the leader to demonstrate his/her commitment to their development by being more of a coach and mentor than boss. Millennials are also looking for ways they can share their expertise and knowledge with other members of the team who need assistance in areas that they are proficient with such as technology. This helps to create a greater partnership with them and makes the millennials feel valuable. Here are a few strategies for implementation in order to help millennials feel you are providing training and development for enhancement and utilization of their knowledge:

- Provide a coach to help the millennials understand how they can utilize their soft-skills training in areas such as workplace culture, working with team members assertively, processing feedback, and creating long-term career goals. Millennials are always looking for ways to be more productive and enhance the quality of their life.

- Allow millennials the opportunity to share their knowledge in the workplace. For example, Allow them to share their knowledge about social networking. This allows them to tap into their strengths and allows everyone to gain from their knowledge.

On-going training and development are the only way each generation will continue to thrive in the new economy.

RETAINING MILLENNIALS

"Coaching is a skill set you need to develop with your leaders because it is the key to retaining talent in your company." – Gary Wilbers

The next seven ways will give you strategies about how you can retain the millennials after you have brought them onboard. These strategies will also enhance your retention rate with other generations if you adopt them throughout your company. The best part of this plan is that you are creating an attraction, retention and engagement strategy which will bring your company into the 21st century.

1. INSPIRE, MOTIVATE, ENCOURAGE

The millennial generation has grown up with collaborative relationships. They will respond favorably to an inspiring, motivating and encouraging leader who recognizes them for their efforts. Remember: Millennials are always asking this question, "What's in it for me?" They want to know why and what the purpose of the task is versus just doing it. Make sure you take time to explain your expectations for the final results of a project or task. If it is a larger project, have follow-up progress points to check their progression. Millennials will respond favorably when they know what is needed and expected.

This generation grew up receiving a toy in their Happy Meal. They were awarded ribbons for participation in sports and activities. The millennials were told they were special and their self-esteem was built up daily. These are some of the reasons leaders need to realize positive feedback is necessary for millennials to be successful. You will need to have a very open and candid conversation with your millennials to find out how they expect feedback to occur. For example, Do they want face-to-face feedback, text messages, email or a combination. The key for any leader is to find out what works for your team and you. When you understand what is needed, it is easier to give the millennials the feedback they are seeking. Understanding their perspective will ultimately save a lot of time.

I learned from sharing coaching strategies with my clients, that the number one thing we all do not do enough of is inspiring, motivating, and encouraging our team. Are you up for a challenge that will make a difference with your employees?

For the next thirty days, I want you to share one inspiring, motivating or encouraging word of praise with each team member. This praise must be sincere, genuine and specific. This means each day you must look for one thing each team member is doing that makes a difference. If you successfully complete this thirty-day challenge, you will see a different viewpoint. After completing the challenge, you will become a different leader, and your team will be more willing to help you achieve your goals. I have given this challenge to numerous people I have coached, and each time they cannot believe the results. After you have success with this challenge, please email me your results at gwilbers@goascend.biz .

2. RECOGNITON

Recognition happens after inspiring, motivating and encouraging your millennials as you acknowledge the efforts they bring to the team. The things we say are millennial driven but apply to everyone you lead in your company. Think about yourself. Do you like to be recognized for your efforts? Yes, it makes us feel good when we know we are appreciated for our work. Make sure you let the millennials know you have their best interest at heart.

Remember to celebrate successes and special occasions with your team. When your team achieves a goal, celebrate that success with a special luncheon or team party. The millennials are used to making a big deal out of their birthdays. I have heard it said before that millennials don't just celebrate their birthday on one specific day; they celebrate it all month. Here are some occasions for celebrating successes:

- Birthday celebrations

- Hiring anniversaries

- Hitting a goal or completion of a major project

- New team member joins your team

- End-of-quarter celebration

- Major holidays

You can create an endless list. Remember: The team that wins together, stays together.

Make sure you get to know each of your team member's personal preference of recognition. Some personality styles like public recognition while some prefer private recognition. The main key is to recognize your team for their contributions. This works for every generation.

3. FLEXIBILITY IN WORK SCHEDULE

According to a recent study, 74% of millennials said they want a flexible work schedule. The same study said, "88% want 'work-life integration'." This isn't the same as work-life balance since work and life now blend together inexplicably. One of the questions you should expect during an interview with a millennial is "How many hours per day will I be expected to work?" They are asking how much time they will need to work in order to do the job.

So ultimately, the key to flexibility in work schedule is one that I would suggest you be willing to change. Evaluate the tasks that employees perform and decide if flexibility can be incorporated. Here are some examples you may be able to put into practice:

- Allow employees the ability to work from home or a remote location as needed.

- Give employees the opportunity to work flexible schedules based on core times (when employees must be at work) and flexible time bands (when employees can vary arrival and departure).

- Offer the ability for employees to work less hours when needed without pay but allow them to keep their benefits.

4. SOCIAL AWARENESS

The millennials want to make an impact on society. They have been raised to feel enormous passion for their environment, communities and global citizens. In part, this is due to them not knowing of a time without internet and wireless phones, which have continuously given them access to events and social networks.

What are the implications of this passion and social awareness? How can you use it to attract a loyal employee? The key strategy is for you to unite their energy and purpose to what your company does for society. Find ways to build relationships in order to find out what is important to them as individuals and then connect the dots to use that energy and passion in your company. If you take the time to get to know the millennials and what is important to them, you will be able to share how the values, vision and mission of your company will allow them to express their social awareness. This takes effort, but if you are willing, you can create an unstoppable employee who will impact your company for years to come.

One of the questions I am asked is "How do you define your company as a cause?" The best suggestion I have is to get your team together and have a millennial facilitate the discussion. Make sure to meet with the facilitator and set up the desired outcomes. Remember: Collaboration will have a huge impact for everyone in your company. Here are some suggestions for guiding your team in developing your company's cause:

- What is your company's value to society?

- What should a good citizen in your industry look like?

- What will your company cause be?

- How will your employees enhance the company's cause?

As you start looking at making your company a "cause" rather than a business, new possibilities will transpire.

5. COACH ME

The best method to lead millennials and have them commit to your company is through coaching and connecting with each of them in their own unique way. Coaching is the number one skill an effective leader can use to create a positive and productive working relationship with the millennials on your team. Millennials are looking for instant and constant feedback and praise about how they are performing. Previous generations were evaluated maybe once or twice a year; this generation expects weekly and sometimes daily feedback. If done in a positive way, this ongoing feedback and coaching will lead to the millennials and your company reaching their goals.

The key to providing the right amount of coaching to your millennial is to have an upfront meeting discussing what he/she expects and how he/she would like this delivered. Remember: The millennial wants to share how he/she would like to receive coaching. This helps a leader find a common ground and an increased relationship with the millennial. Most millennials are seeking tips about how to think strategically and want you to share aspects of the business and expectations needed for success. In creating these expectations, make sure you are very clear, specific and detailed about the metrics because the millennials will keep score and expect you to do the same.

As you work with millennials, make sure you provide support with engaging them in the workplace. When they become engaged, they will be more effective and productive. Here are few ways you can help the millennials become more engaged in the workplace:

- Encouragement – share the positive results they are bringing to the company.

- Explain your intentions – discuss what you want and why you want them to succeed.

- Boundaries – provide clear and concise expectations and specific rules for internet, phone usage, meetings, dress code, etc.

- Lead by example –model good behavior as millennials want consistency and will pay attention to your words and actions.

- Have fun –praise, recognize and celebrate accomplishments with your team.

These five strategies will work for any generation. The more you share with your team, the more you will see your team become engaged. This is critical. A recent 2015 Gallup survey suggested that workplace engagement is at less than 33%. That means out of ten workers only three of them are engaged. Think about the effect that has on your team.

6. ONBOARDING

Onboarding is defined as "to bring someone new to the group or company into the mainstream; to support the process for a new hire to fully integrate and function in his/her role or position." Bringing a millennial onboard quickly provides a faster transition to becoming productive. Onboarding millennials is crucial for you to retain them. The millennial is anxious to begin. Make sure you are ready for him/her to make meaningful connections with your company. He/she wants to know how your company works and what his/her role is. This will make the millennial more productive and allows him/her to connect to others. As you share his/her workspace, give him/her some authority to customize. Remember: Millennials want to be able to express themselves. They are looking for you to breakdown their work into steps and have the defined processes ready for them to follow. Start with sharing a detailed 90-day expectations plan, and then let them help devise a strategy that will allow them to achieve this plan. Be ready to listen to great suggestions from them about how they can be attained. Make sure you are respectful, and do not say, "We tried that, but it didn't work." By creating a 90-day plan, you will engage them quickly in your company, help them become connected, and allow them to immediately become productive.

As you add millennials to your team, make sure to talk with them about the community service and social connections your company participates in.

They will want to know what causes you support and why. This is a great time to find out what they are passionate about, and how they will help with the causes your company supports. Some companies create mentor/buddy relationships that help the millennials not only in transitioning into their new role but also involving them in the company's social causes. Millennials want to give back. When they have a chance to do that as part of the job, it will create a win-win for all.

7. TRANSPARENCY

One selective trait you will find with millennials is they are very transparent both in their personal and professional lives. Remember: They grew up with the internet providing information at all times. The vast amount of information existing online and with social networks has allowed them to completely research you and your company. The first day the millennial walks into your company, he/she already knows about your company.

Because of this millennials have lots of questions and great ideas that they want to discuss with you. Listen to their ideas and ask for further explanation.

Remember: Being transparent about the good/bad in your company will engage the millennials to help find ways benefiting all.

COPYRIGHT: <A HREF="HTTPS://WWW.123RF.COM/PROFILE_RYANKING999">RYANKING999 / 123RF STOCK PHOTO</A>

ENGAGING MILLENNIALS

"Engagement is attained when you connect employees with the work they do." – Gary Wilbers

The last seven ways are how to engage millennials in your workplace. According to a 2015 Gallup survey less than 33% of any workforce is engaged. The challenge is to find ways to engage not only millennials but all generations.

1. TECHNOLOGY

Millennials are accustomed to having a computer and seeking information from Google or other search engines. They are so much more proficient in using technology to help them achieve more in a shorter amount of time.

The key to engaging millennials is to embrace their tech-savviness and use it to help the company move forward. For example, you might create a technology committee and have a millennial from your team and one of your other leaders co-chair. Allow them to explore ways your company could use technology to streamline some operations and customer service making your company stand out.

Do you realize the impact gaming has had on millennials? They grew up playing video games. Today most games create endings that change based on the decisions made by the player, which impacts the locus of control, a person's belief about how much power one has over the events in his/her life. Gaming has taught millennials to use a complex set of decision-making skills and multiple pieces of data to make decisions quickly. To them learning will closely resemble gaming, and it becomes a trial-and-error approach to solving problems. Technology is the tool they prefer to use to solve problems.

This also has led millennials to be multi-taskers because they are used to having several responsibilities and working on several projects simultaneously. The key for the leader of millennials is to coach him/her about what is most important and what is expected to finalize the project.

2. COMMUNICATION

Communication with any generation is the number one workplace challenge. Lack of communication creates lost productivity and employee conflict. Millennials expect a form of "helicopter management" style. They want their leaders to hover over them in order to help and keep them pointed in the right direction. Millennials are used to a close adult figure in their life and expect a similar style of management. The challenge is millennials want more of a coach/mentor than a boss. As we have discussed before, they seek out constant feedback and recognition. The key for this coach is to find out how they want to receive communication and feedback. Each team member will be different. Many millennials prefer text or instant messaging.

When you are handing out projects and/or assignments, one word of caution is to make sure you communicate to them why completion is important. Millennials resent being handed busywork with no explanation of its purpose. The key is to take time to explain how this work impacts and leads to specific results for the projects and/or assignments. Use the eight pillars of communication when you are trying to get your message across:

- Precision
- Connections
- Packaged
- Clear
- Empathy
- Transparency
- Fact-based
- Respect

Using these basic principles, you are setting a firm foundation in order to build communication with others. These eight pillars are explained in detail in my book <u>The High Achiever Leadership Formula.</u> You can order this from Amazon or go to <u>www.goascend.biz/getmycopy</u>.

Another way to combat the loss of content is to employ active listening in your communication. It is a way of listening causing the person to often hear messages that are generally missed. Active listening has five basic ingredients to help the listener assimilate and retain all that is being said:

- No distractions

- Body language

- Clarity

- No evaluating

- Respectful response

Active listening is a vital trait a leader in today's fast paced business environment needs to develop. The challenge we all face is taking the time to truly listen and be present during our conversations. Communication is vital for engaging the millennial worker in your company.

3. TEAMWORK

Millennials understand the value of working with a team of people and enjoy collaborating with others because they have grown up with the idea of teamwork. Since they were young, adults have shared a belief system with them that everyone should participate and be included. This mindset becomes a culture heritage that millennials have carried with them to the workforce. When they participated in events, everyone had a chance to compete. This is where the belief system comes from that participation rewards are part of the process. When they enter the workforce, they are looking for recognition for their contribution to the team.

From a recent study of millennials: 88% prefer a collaborative work culture rather than a competitive one. This is the type of environment a millennial expects. Millennials believe it doesn't matter what your title and rank are in the company. To them all of the team is on the same level. Collaboration and communication are key components. They're comfortable asking for advice and used to getting responses quickly. Leaders must create an atmosphere which enhances this type of teamwork and creative collaboration.

4. GET TO KNOW ME

The one trait all great leaders have in common is building relationships with their people. One of the number one traits millennials are looking for in their leader is the willingness to know them for who they are. Some of the best leaders will create relationships based on these principles:

- Connect with who they are and their passions in both their professional and personal life.

- Coach them about learning, developing and creating experiences that will help develop skills not just business processes.

- Help them understand the work purpose and how it impacts the company.

- Create a culture of fun within the work environment.

- Allow them to connect to the boss.

A question to ask yourself is "Do you really know your team?" If not, begin connecting with your team on their level.

5. BUSINESS ACUMEN

Acumen is defined as "quick insight or the ability to make accurate judgments of people or situations, especially as they relate to business." Millennials come to us with strong technical skills and multi-tasking abilities, but lack business acumen. Remember: You probably did not come with these skills either; it is a skill that improves over the course of time.

Effective business acumen skills generally start with a professional manner and attitude. Helping millennials effectively build business relationships is one of the foundation components of this. The key to understanding business acumen is for the employee to know what is expected of him/her. Here are some topics for discussion:

- Explain business acumen

- Share culture of the company

- Describe the employee's role in the company

- Discuss your company's available resources

- Talk about punctuality/attendance, performance expectations, and business etiquette

- Help them accept criticism

6. MILLENNIAL TEAM COMMITTEE

What can your company do now to help everyone understand your workplace dynamics? Many large companies are creating millennial team committees to understand the millennial generation, which will be the largest generation in the workforce in the next several years. This committee should consist of members from your leadership team and currently employed millennials. The goal of the committee is to serve as an educational resource and promote awareness. Understanding the differences of characteristics and culture, will empower and support your team with the realization of how to handle the uniqueness of each generation.

This committee could also explore ways the company needs to adjust and change to allow flexibility in order to meet the demands of this workforce. I highly recommend you survey your millennial team about what they want in terms of benefits, flexibility in work schedules, technology, etc. This will identify the business functions that need to change in order to increase the attraction, retention and engagement of millennial talent. Remember: Business is about changing, adopting and moving to the direction of your customers. Your employees are your internal customers. They decide if your business succeeds or not.

7. PASSION

The one thing that drives the millennial generation is their passion. When you determine how you can engage that passion, you will find loyalty and commitment to your company. Remember: Millennials have high expectations about their competence and have been encouraged to follow their passion. They fully expect meaningful work, flexible hours and work-life integration. How will your company encourage this passion? Here are a few suggestions for engagement of the millennials' passion:

- During the interview process specifically address their passion.

- Share your company's opportunities to give back to the community.

- Discuss with the millennial which opportunity appeals to their passion.

- During the onboarding process involve the millennial in ways to serve the community.

- Survey your team about additional ways your company could serve others.

- Allow your employees a certain number of hours per month to help with nonprofit causes.

- Try to match your employees with other employees who share similar passions.

When you take the time to find out what your employees are passionate about and tap into that resource, it will create loyalty within your company.

CONCLUSION

"The world is passing through troublous times. The young people of today think of nothing but themselves. They have no reverence for parents or old age. They are impatient of all restraint. They talk as if they knew everything, and what passes for wisdom with us is foolishness with them"
-Peter the Hermit, 1274

When we started this book, I stated that the challenge today is not the millennial worker but how we decide to view this generation. Each generation has had trade-offs. As I did my research about the millennials, I realized they are different from me, but they are not lazy, entitled and narcissistic. Every generation tends to say this about the next generation. All generations want similar things. This group is bold enough to demand it.

During a recent training I was doing for a company, fifteen of the managers were learning about the millennial generation. It was apparent that some of the managers were frustrated with the issues of this generation. On the other hand, a few of the managers were finding success by implementing many of the concepts I shared with you in this book. The number one factor that made a difference: The manager had to be willing to try to find ways to attract, retain and engage the millennial in the workplace. Is this a 100% success? No, but the managers realized if their actions changed from being manager to coach, they would be successful.

My final suggestion is to ask yourself: "What is the paradigm I have for the millennial generation?" Paradigm is defined as "the way we see, understand, and interpret the world; our mental map." The way you view this generation will determine how you decide to respond. My hope is that this book has given you a new way to view the millennial generation. It is vital for you and your business to realize the potential the millennials will bring to your company. Your future success depends on this generation.

Make it a GREAT day!

Gary Wilbers

"Every generation is unique and challenging in their own way. The question is: 'How can I embrace the strengths they bring to the workplace?'." – Gary Wilbers

CITATIONS & REFERENCES

Asghar, R. (2014, January 14). What Millennials Want In The Workplace (And Why You Should Start Giving It To Them). Retrieved March 16, 2017, from https://www.forbes.com/sites/robasghar/2014/01/13/what-millennials-want-in-the-workplace-and-why-you-should-start-giving-it-to-them/#15c4e8744c40

Gallup, I. (2016, January 13). Employee Engagement in U.S. Stagnant in 2015. Retrieved March 16, 2017, from http://www.gallup.com/poll/188144/employee-engagement-stagnant-2015.aspx

M. (2017, January 20). How Much Time Do People Spend on Social Media? [Infographic]. Retrieved March 16, 2017, from http://www.socialmediatoday.com/marketing/how-much-time-do-people-spend-social-media-infographic

ABOUT THE AUTHOR

Ascend Business Strategies began because Gary wanted better training with more complete Human Resources and Leadership Development opportunities for his companies. Through its early development stage, it became very evident this was soon to be a company that could help other businesses with training resources designed for practical use and address what is not commonly taught in business management schools. The desire to help others develop and become better launched a national business based in the heart of Missouri.

Leadership Training | Coaching | Speaking | Sales Training

To learn more about coaching, keynote speaking, and our unique training programs, contact Ascend Business Strategies at goascend.biz or (866) 549-0434.

Gary Wilbers is a coach, speaker, trainer and author. He works with companies to transform the challenges leaders and teams face in regards to change and growth. Gary has been a successful entrepreneur and owner of multiple businesses in Missouri since 1990. He studied entrepreneurs such as Sam Walton, Brendon Burchard, Brian Tracy, and Charles Red Scott. He learned their principles and then built his own roadmap for success which he shares as he helps leaders develop into High Achievers.

HOW TO CONTACT GARY

For more information on Coaching, Training, and Keynote Speaking, contact Gary and the Ascend Team:

Phone: (573) 644-6655 or (866) 549-0434
Email: GWilbers@GoAscend.biz
Online: www.goascend.biz

Gary Wilbers
1731 Elm Court
Jefferson City, MO 65101

Subscribe to Gary's weekly video blog:
www.goascend.biz/blog/

To purchase bulk copies of this book at a discounted rate, please contact Gary Wilbers:
gwilbers@goascend.biz or (573) 644-6655

www.ingramcontent.com/pod-product-compliance
Lightning Source LLC
Chambersburg PA
CBHW061449180526
45170CB00004B/1624